The Nightmare World
of the Shark

THE NIGHTMARE

WORLD OF THE SHARK

By Joseph J. Cook and William L. Wisner

Illustrated with photographs and diagrams

DODD, MEAD & COMPANY · NEW YORK

ACKNOWLEDGMENTS

The authors particularly wish to thank the following people and institutions for helping to make this book possible: Dr. Perry W. Gilbert, Professor of Zoology at Cornell University, Ithaca, New York; Dr. John Clark, President, American Littoral Society, Sandy Hook Marine Laboratory, Highlands, New Jersey; John Casey, Narragansett Marine Game Fish Laboratory, United States Bureau of Sport Fisheries and Wildlife; Captain Frank Mundus of the *Cricket II*, Montauk, New York; the Alaska State Museum; the New York Zoological Society; Marineland of Florida; the Consulate General Offices of New Zealand and Australia; the Oceanographic Research Institute of Durban, Republic of South Africa; and The American Museum of Natural History, New York City, for permission to reprint their photographs.

97517

Library of Congress Catalog Card Number: 68-29808

Printed in the United States of America

In warm appreciation of his friendship,
this book is dedicated to DR. ROSS F. NIGRELLI,
Director of the New York Aquarium and
Osborn Marine Laboratory

Introduction

Sharks hold a unique place in the sea kingdom. Among fishes they are the oldest inhabitants of the hydrosphere. Their tribe includes the largest fishes in the world, as well as those most dangerous to man. Because sharks are so fascinating and dangerous, they are the target of intense scientific study. More than two hundred scientists around the world are working to learn their secrets and to predict their moods. Cautious by nature, the sleek and efficient creatures usually avoid clumsy human intruders, but occasionally they attack with ferocity. Scientists want to know why, not only for their own information but also for the safety of swimmers, divers, and sailors all over the globe.

This is a book to bring you up to date on shark knowledge, fact by fact.

John Clark, President
American Littoral Society
Sandy Hook Marine Laboratory
Highlands, New Jersey

Contents

I. The Far-flung World of the Shark

A warm afternoon on San Francisco's Bakers Beach brought tragic death from a shark's jaws to a young swimmer, soon after two teen-agers ran across the sand, dashed into the surf, and plunged headlong into a breaking wave.

The two swimmers splashed seaward, the boy far in the lead. About 150 feet offshore, he suddenly stopped swimming and began to tread water. He had spotted an ugly fin cutting through the water. "It's a shark!" he called to the girl. "Get out of here!"

The shark circled slowly, then hurled its huge body clear of the water. The terrified boy saw that it was a monster, at least ten feet long. Then the animal charged at him.

An instant later the water foamed red with blood. The boy screamed and signaled to the girl to swim to shore. But she ignored his warning and splashed toward the shark, hoping to scare it off. Suddenly, with a flick of its powerful tail, the great fish vanished into the sea.

Adult female sand shark, sometimes called sand tiger, on the prowl

New York Zoological Society Photo

The girl put her arms around her companion and towed him back to the beach. But he had lost a great deal of blood and died less than three hours later. The girl was awarded the Young American Medal for Bravery by President John F. Kennedy for this extraordinary display of courage.

Ever since man first ventured into the sea he has been the victim of shark attacks. Through the ages these animals have been man's most feared enemy in the oceans of the world. Even today man stands in awe and fear of the shark.

There was a time, about 500 million years ago, when no sharks swam the warm seas that covered much of the earth. Invertebrates, animals without backbones, roamed the sea in these early years of life on our planet. Animals that had a skeleton at all had it on the outside of their body, as is true today of shrimp, crabs, and lobsters.

Approximately 350 million years ago, sharks made their first appearance in the sea. Primitive ancestors of today's sharks glided in and out of the shadows of prehistoric seas millions of years before the first human creatures walked the land. Those early sharks were preying on smaller fishes even before the first trees appeared and even before the giant dinosaurs ruled the earth.

Sharks are members of the ancient class of Elasmobranchii, order Selachii, and are related to the rays, skates, torpedoes (electric rays), a strange-looking sea resident known as the sawfish, and another odd-appearing fish called the chimaera. They are among the most primitive of any living vertebrates. During those 350 million years, they pursued a lonely course down the road of evolution, meeting the problem of changing conditions by changing scarcely at all. Sharks truly remained prehistoric monsters as they terrorized the sea through countless years.

Whatever scattered fragments of knowledge scientists have been able to gather about prehistoric sharks have come from fossil beds, the cemeteries of animals which died millions of years ago and were imbedded permanently in layers of rock and mineral. Primitive creatures of many kinds, small and large, died and settled to the bottom of the water in which they lived. There their remains were trapped in mud or other materials which eventually became rock. The animals' entombed bodies literally turned to stone, too, and so were preserved forevermore, perhaps to be dug up by fossil hunters countless centuries later.

Most of the fishes with which we are familiar are classified as Teleostei, or bony fishes. They have skeletons of bone. But sharks are different. They belong to another group classified by ichthyologists, or students of fishes, as cartilaginous fishes. The internal framework or skeleton of this type of fish is composed entirely of cartilage, the substance which in humans forms the framework of the ears and nose. Since the skeletons are cartilage, not bone, these fishes do not lend themselves readily to fossilization. As a result, in most instances, the only remains of prehistoric sharks are their teeth. Being hard, these fossilize and endure.

We know that some of the prehistoric sharks were nightmarish creatures, much larger than their modern descendants. The late Captain William E. Young, lifelong hunter and student of sharks, possessed a fossilized shark tooth the size of a man's hand. Captain Young theorized its owner could have been one hundred feet long

Front view of the Port Jackson shark which has remained relatively unchanged for 181 million years

with a mouth large enough to accommodate a rowboat with a six-foot man standing up in it. Captain Frank Mundus, of Montauk, New York, a shark-fishing skipper-guide, possesses a large fossilized tooth. Carbon tests, by which scientists can determine the age of an ancient object, revealed that tooth to be at least 100 million years old. The shark which carried it was at least fifty feet long. At the American Museum of Natural History in New York, scientists reconstructed the jaws of a prehistoric shark whose gaping mouth could have held six men standing up in it.

Except for a general decrease in size, among some species at least, sharks have changed relatively little down through the ages. In this respect they are, in a manner of speaking, living fossils. This remote age of the shark family is indicated today in general through examinations of species such as the present Port Jackson shark, which goes back 181 million years; the cow shark, traced back 166 million years; and the cat shark, with a 136-million-year history. By comparison of the teeth of these present-day sharks with the fossilized fangs of their prehistoric ancestors, scientists have been able to deduce that the species have undergone comparatively few changes through the ages. It is with the aid of such comparisons of teeth that we are able to visualize prehistoric sharks, despite the fact that they left us no other remains.

Perhaps most remarkable of all is the fact that sharks have persisted through so many millions of years. Dinosaurs appeared on the earth, then vanished into oblivion, unable to survive in a changing environment. Great changes took place in the sea and on land. Thousands upon thousands of other kinds of sea and land animals appeared, prospered, and then died out. Yet the shark, perhaps due to its bold and active make-up, survived almost without any evolutionary change.

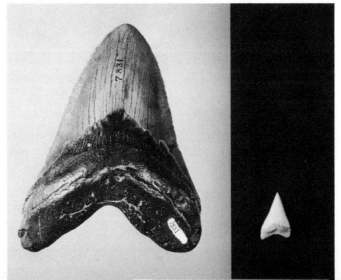

Far left: A fossilized tooth 100 million years old in the hand of a 16-year-old boy

Left: Tooth comparison of a prehistoric shark with the same present day shark

American Museum of Natural History

2. The Shark

Scientists have identified about 250 species of sharks. One species, found in the Gulf of Mexico, is nine inches long, while two other species may reach lengths of sixty feet. However, these larger sharks, which are the largest fish in the sea, have minute teeth and live mainly on small planktonic animals, small squid, and small, schooling fish.

The typical shark is one of the most beautifully streamlined of all fishes. Shaped. like a cigar or torpedo, it is capable of quick bursts of speed which aid it in capturing prey.

The skin of sharks is quite different from that of other fishes. In the first place it is extremely tough. Secondly, instead of the usual scales found on fishes, shark skin carries uncountable thousands of tiny "teeth" known as dermal denticles. The term "dermal denticle" literally means "skin teeth." Actually, these are not teeth at all, but a specialized form of scales. Dermal denticles take different shapes according to

This sand shark illustrates the torpedo-like shape of the typical shark

Marineland of Florida

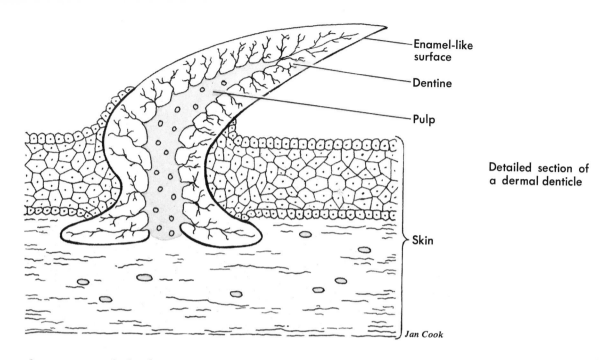

Enamel-like surface

Dentine

Pulp

Detailed section of a dermal denticle

Skin

Jan Cook

the species of shark. Some are shaped like little thorns, others are more flat, with ridges, but none of them resemble the scales we are accustomed to seeing on fishes. All are imbedded in the skin. They are so tiny they can best be seen with a magnifying glass.

If you rub your hand along a shark's hide in the direction of the tail, its dermal denticles are pushed down and the skin feels smooth. If you move your hand in the opposite direction, it rubs against the dermal denticles and they resist. Now the shark's skin feels as rough as coarse sandpaper. These tiny, razor-sharp, close-set denticles can flay a swimmer with a single sideways swipe of the long body.

All true sharks have two sets of paired fins and a backbone of gristle which does not stop at the tail. Rather it extends into the tail itself and supports the upper part. The tail is usually notched and the upper part is longer than the lower part. A powerful, propulsive instrument, the odd-looking tail makes it easy to recognize a shark. The paired fins are fixed and relatively inflexible. They are used mainly for steering, for the shark is incapable of stopping short or backing up and attacks its prey in wild, swerving lunges.

Shark profile

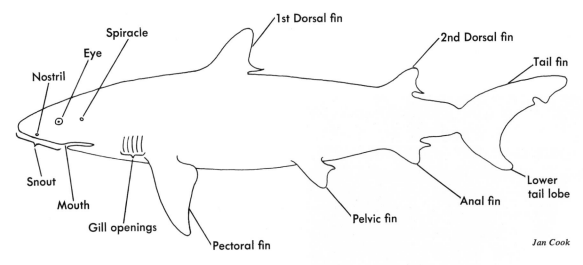

Jan Cook

While bony fishes have only a single gill on each side of the head, sharks have five to seven slits or gill openings on each side. A diminished gill opening called the spiracle is found in some sharks just behind the eye.

The spiracle appears as a small aperture, fitted with a nonreturn valve which opens and closes as the fish breathes. The shark takes in water through its mouth or through the spiracle hole and the water then passes over the gills, supplying the shark with oxygen, and goes through the gill slits.

Another feature characteristic of sharks is the so-called spiral valve in the intestine. Actually, the spiral valve is an attempt to increase the absorptive surface of the intestine, which is much shorter than those of most vertebrates. A ten-foot shark, for example, has only nine feet of intestine, by comparison with twenty-five feet in a six-foot man. Though it varies in shape in different species, the spiral valve is built generally on the principle of a circular ramp, or, when more tightly closed, a series

A shark has an unlimited supply of teeth throughout its life. Here several reserve rows of teeth lie against the inner surface of the jaw. These will migrate outward to replace the upright functional teeth.

Marineland of Florida

of spiraling scrolls one inside the other, with the food passing through the spirals in the process of digestion. Since it may have as many as forty-five turns, the absorptive surface provided within a rather limited space is quite impressive.

Many kinds of fishes have a swim or air bladder. This sac of gas inside their bodies helps them to float and enables them to pause in their swimming without sinking or rising. Since sharks do not have this air bladder they must literally sink or swim. However, a shark is not completely without help in staying afloat, even though it lacks an air bladder. Sharks have very large livers. Sometimes the liver, which is full of oil, may weigh as much as one-tenth of the entire body. Since oil is much lighter than water, the oil-filled liver gives the shark some extra lift and helps make up for the lack of an air sac. Also, some species of shark overcome this lack by gulping air into the stomach. Occasionally, when captured or seeking deeper water, they expel the trapped air forcefully in a prolonged belch, an action that may be the basis for ancient accounts of the roaring of sharks.

The shark's mouth is grim and usually crescent shaped below its long snout, curved backward in a seemingly savage snarl. Inside the well-developed, hinged jaws are rows upon rows of teeth for seizing, cutting, piercing, or crunching. The teeth are arranged in rows around the jaws and there may be more than a single row in use at one time. Behind the functional row or rows are several reserve rows of teeth lying flat against the inner surface of the jaws, like shingles on a roof, all pointing backward. These reserve rows will come into use to replace the outer functional rows which are periodically shed. Replacement occurs by a migration forward

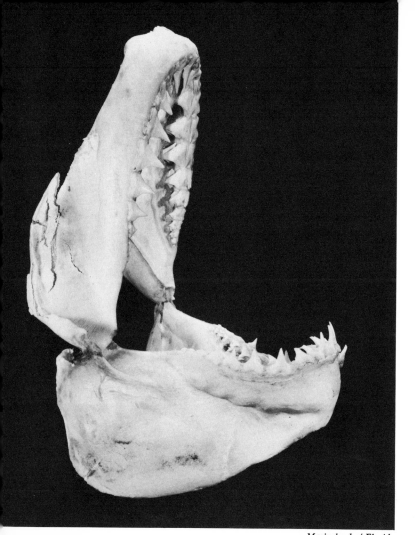

Left: Great white shark jaws

Below: Jaws of the mako shark

of the strong membrane to which the teeth are attached. This process of replacement of teeth continues as long as the shark lives.

Teeth vary in shape, size, and number among sharks. The edges of the teeth vary among shark species, too. Some are smooth while others carry serrations, each of which is a cutting edge in itself.

The shark's teeth are his feeding equipment, and they also are fearsome weapons in defense and offense. Aided by strong jaws, the teeth can inflict frightful damage. Contrary to popular belief, however, it is not so much the power of the jaws that does the damage as it is a combination of biting action (which punctures, cuts, and tears) and a shaking of the shark's head.

Sharks are prowlers, more or less constantly on the search for food, yet they can and do get enough to eat, and generally do not try to cram more food into their stomach when they already have had enough. In this respect sharks are more "sportsmanlike" than certain other marine creatures. Bluefish, for example, are notorious killers of smaller fishes. Bluefish will attack a panic-stricken school of prey, fill their stomachs, then vomit the contents and fill them all over again.

It is true that some sharks are voracious and that some, like the tiger shark, will swallow odd items at times. However, for the most part, sharks are fish-eaters, varying their diets with squids, shrimp, crabs of various kinds and lesser sea creatures. If sufficiently hungry they are not above eating each other. Their diets also depend in great measure upon whether or not they are bottom feeders by nature, or prowl through the sea's intermediate levels, or frequently travel near the surface.

From many years of experience as a shark sportsfishing skipper, Captain Frank Mundus observes that sharks follow schools of fishes, seizing those that lag behind or are crippled or slower swimmers. Like people, perhaps sharks like to do things the easy way whenever possible. At the same time this may be a part of nature's way of eliminating the weak, the sick, and the unfit.

It has been observed that smaller fishes seem to be able to sense when there is no danger from a shark. Ordinarily, food fishes such as mackerel hurry off when a shark appears. Yet there are times when they have been seen to remain and simply open a corridor in their midst to let the predator through. In such intrusions, it has been theorized, the smaller fishes sense that the prowler is not hungry and that they therefore have nothing to fear from him. Similar instances are well known in the animal world. Zebra and other prey of lions will continue grazing astonishingly close to the giant cats at times, apparently sensing that the predators have eaten and will not attack them.

Opposite: A good view of a remora attached to a sand shark. The remora holds on by means of suction disks. It is not a parasite but travels along "for the ride."
Marineland of Florida

Right: Excellent view of the sucking disks by which a remora attaches itself to a shark
Marineland of Florida

This 2,500-pound maneater was in the process of making a meal out of one of his brothers which had been hooked by a Fremantle, Australia, fisherman. The twenty-foot white shark was caught subsequently.

London Daily Express

It is interesting that often a shark carries several "hitchhikers" around with him. The remora, or shark sucker, is a fish from two to three feet long with a sucking disk on its head by which it clings to sharks and other large fishes. The remora is not a parasite but merely partakes of the scraps from its host's food.

There are great gaps in scientists' knowledge of what sharks can see. The eyes, set far apart on either side of the head, are seemingly fixed in a cold stare. At one time sharks' eyes were belived to be of little use, but recently it has been discovered that their eyes are very sensitive. They are not good at seeing fine detail, but can easily detect differences in light and darkness. This may explain why sharks are attracted to light or shiny objects.

Scientists do know that sharks are "smell minded." Smell is one of the most important senses by which sharks find out what is going on in their world.

What about other senses? Spearfishermen have noticed that sharks sometimes suddenly appear as a speared fish struggles in the water. The fish may not be bleeding, or at least there has not been enough time for the blood to spread far in the water. Undoubtedly, sharks can detect vibrations in the water caused by a struggling fish. Many a marlin, tuna, or other gamefish has been attacked and mangled by a shark while still being played by an angler. Divers have been able to drive sharks away by shouting at them underwater. Some sounds, however, attract sharks. Answers to these questions may come from studies going on at the Lerner Marine Laboratory, a field station of the American Museum of Natural History in the Bahamas.

To perpetuate the species some sharks have their young by laying eggs which are

protected from other marine animals by a horny shell. However, most sharks bear live young which are called pups.

Down through the ages sharks have survived by remaining primitive creatures and it is this primitive, savage, primeval force of the shark that even today intrigues and awes man.

A catch of "blue dogs," readily identified by their slender bodies and unusually long pectoral fins

Cecil Clovelly

3. A Varied Family

Modern sharks comprise a large tribe, encountered in oceans all over the globe, from the cold waters of the polar regions to the warm, turquoise seas of the tropics. Theirs is a varied family whose members come in a wide assortment of sizes.

Among the family's very smallest members are species of little sharks known as dogfishes. There are several kinds of these, identified variously as the smooth, spiny, black, chain, and piked dogfishes. Typical of the group is the smooth dogfish that ranges from Cape Cod, Massachusetts, all the way down to Uruguay and southern Brazil.

The smooth dogfish grows to a length of three to four feet, and once in a great while there will be one that is five feet long. The smooth dogfish is completely harmless. He could not inflict a bite if he wanted to, because his teeth are extremely small. Like most other dogfishes, these little sharks are hated by surf anglers and commercial fishermen because they steal bait intended for more desirable fishes.

Commercial fishermen also dislike them because they eat fishes caught in nets and can even damage the nets.

In the medium-sized class of sharks, the blue shark, attaining lengths of at least eleven or twelve feet, is a common species. Nicknamed "blue dog," he gets his name from his beautiful blue color. On the back this color is a dark indigo blue, which becomes a bright blue along the sides and finally gives way to a snow white on the underside.

Blue sharks are distributed throughout many waters of the world, including the Mediterranean Sea, the coasts of Europe, and tropical western Africa. They also have been reported in the vast Indo-Pacific region, including South Africa and Australia. Blue sharks are encountered from California on down to Mexico, and along the North and South American coasts of the Atlantic Ocean from Nova Scotia to Brazil.

The blue shark is characterized by a very slender body. He is, in fact, one of the most slender of sharks. He is so slim that he can bend in a flash and bite his own tail or the hand of anyone who happens to be holding it. The blue shark also is characterized by his long pectoral fins, proportionately larger than those of many other kinds of sharks. Those pectorals, coupled with the blue's color and his peculiar eel-like swimming motion, a kind of wiggle, enable anglers to identify this fish in the water.

One of the larger medium-size sharks is the dusky. This husky brute attains lengths up to ten and eleven feet, possibly to fourteen feet, and weights of five hundred pounds or more. His color is a bluish or leaden gray on the back and upper sides. On

Model of a whale shark, largest of all fishes

American Museum of Natural History

the lower sides this becomes a lighter shade of the same color, then fades away to white on the belly or underside.

Duskies have rather wide distribution in warm-temperate and tropical seas. On the United States' eastern coast they are encountered quite commonly between Cape Cod, Massachusetts, and New Jersey. Actually, these sharks are found on both sides of the Atlantic Ocean, although scientists are not yet certain if those in United States waters are exactly the same species as those reported for such locations as the Mediterranean coast of Spain and Table Bay, South Africa. Scattered reports tell of duskies in the Gulf of Mexico off Louisiana, along the North American seaboard from Canada's Maritime Provinces to southern Florida, in the Bahama Islands, and all the way down to Brazil.

The largest sharks of all are the whale shark and the basking shark. Not only are they the kings of the shark family for size, they are the very largest of all fishes.

The whale shark, so called because of his enormous size and not because of any relationship to whales, is a huge creature, with lengths reported to reach sixty feet and more. Specimens up to forty-five feet are on record, as are several in the 30- to 34-foot class. Often when whale sharks are harpooned and brought into port there are no scales strong enough to hold them, so their bulk must be estimated. It is not known how much a 60-foot giant would weigh, but you can get some idea of their bulk from the fact that a 38-foot specimen brought ashore in Florida was estimated at 26,594 pounds, or more than thirteen tons.

Whale sharks are essentially a tropical species, inhabiting or visiting warm seas all over the globe in such widely separated places as Japan, the Gulf of California, South Africa, Brazil, the Bay of Bengal, the Bahamas, the Philippines, and the Gulf of Mexico. They also straggle into warm-temperate areas occasionally, and have been known to stray as far north as Long Island, New York.

They are inoffensive, easy-going leviathans who are content to feed on small fishes and tiny marine animals, cruising through the seas with their mouths open to suck in food like giant vacuum cleaners. Despite whale sharks' huge bulk, their

At Massaua, Ethiopia, in the 1930's, a whale shark hangs over the side of the S. S. *Francesco Crispi* after a collision with the ship at sea

American Museum of Natural History

teeth are astonishingly minute and the big creatures are quite harmless to humans. The only possible damage from them, and it is remote, stems from their sluggish nature and habit of lazing at the sea's surface. Under such circumstances a boat might collide with one and conceivably suffer damage.

The basking shark is the second-largest member of the shark family. Credited with lengths to fifty feet and represented in records by 40- and 45-foot specimens, this species rivals but does not match the whale shark for size. Here again the fish are so large that weighing them poses a problem, and precise weights for the larger specimens are not available. On record, however, are those smaller basking sharks captured off Monterey, California. One, a 28-footer, weighed in at 6,850 pounds. The other, just inches short of thirty feet, showed 8,600 pounds on the scale. From these weights it can be seen that the basking shark falls far short of equaling the whale shark in sheer bulk. Even so, he has the distinction of being the world's second-largest fish.

The basking shark also is sluggish, inoffensive, and harmless to man. He too dines on minute marine creatures, swimming leisurely along with his mouth open to scoop them in. Also like the whale shark, his teeth are extremely small, measuring only a fraction of an inch long. And again like the whale shark, he often lolls at the surface of the sea, his dorsal fin and snout showing, presumably enjoying the sun's warmth. At times he also feeds at the surface. The basking shark has little fear of boats, a courage that is his undoing if there happen to be shark hunters in the area.

The enormously long gill slits of the basking shark set him apart from all other

The enormously long gill slits of the basking shark are plainly visible inside and outside of this specimen

American Museum of Natural History

The white shark can grow to a monster size of thirty-six feet. This specimen shows the stout build of the maneater.

Marineland of Florida

sharks. His color is dull gray above while the underside may be the same color or lighter than the back.

Unlike whale sharks, basking sharks favor cooler waters. Their distribution includes temperate and colder zones of the Atlantic and Pacific Oceans. It is not yet certain that they all comprise exactly the same species, but it can be said that basking sharks are represented on the western seaboard of North America from California to British Columbia, and on the Atlantic Coast from Newfoundland to North Carolina. The many other regions throughout the world which play host to basking sharks in varying numbers include the eastern side of the Atlantic from Iceland southward to the Mediterranean and Morocco, the South Atlantic Ocean off South Africa and Argentina, the South Pacific Ocean along the coasts of Peru and Ecuador, as well as the waters of New Zealand and Australia.

The third largest shark and the third largest fish in all the world is the white shark, commonly known as the "maneater." Twenty to 21-footers have been recorded, and there is one monster on record as approximately 36-feet long. It has been repeated frequently that the white shark probably attains lengths of forty feet; but this has yet to be proved.

Distributed widely throughout tropical and warm-temperate seas, white sharks are moderately stout-bodied fish and their weights are correspondingly great. A 21-footer captured in Cuban waters weighed 7,100 pounds. What 30- to 36-foot specimens would weigh we can only guess, but it seems safe to say that their bulk could go up to 10,000 pounds or more.

The weight of any shark depends upon his girth. That girth, in turn, depends upon his general physical condition, and specifically upon the health of his liver. A healthy liver is an enormous organ in a shark. To give you some idea, the liver of that 7,100-pounder caught in Cuban waters weighed 1,005 pounds.

A white shark's color varies greatly. The back and upper sides can be a lead gray, almost black on some individuals, and bluish gray or brownish gray on others. The underside is invariably a dirty white. Some specimens are a lead white all over.

The white shark devours its prey practically intact as illustrated by the presence of sea lions, seals, and other sharks up to seven feet long in the stomachs of some specimens.

Many years ago, the great American naturalist William T. Hornaday declared his belief that the only man-eating species is the white shark. Since then it has been proved that several kinds of sharks are man-eaters, at least on occasion.

Tiger sharks are especially dreaded as killers in the West Indies and Australia. Lengths of twelve and thirteen feet and weights to 1,300 pounds are not rare for tigers. Drs. Henry B. Bigelow and William C. Schroeder tell of one measuring fifteen feet, two inches, which was caught off South Carolina, and another specimen of eighteen feet caught off Cuba. It has been stated that the maximum size for tiger sharks is thirty feet.

The tiger shark has a gray or grayish brown color which fades on the sides and belly. Dark spots on the back fuse into irregular stripes on the sides and fins.

The swift, powerful, and extremely active mako is another shark considered po-

The notched teeth of this brute identify him as a tiger shark

Pictorial Parade

tentially dangerous. These sharks, distributed widely throughout the tropical and warm-temperate zones of the Atlantic and Pacific Oceans, attain lengths to twelve feet and known weights to at least one thousand pounds. The deep blue-gray color on the top of the mako's body changes to snow white on the underside and the large mouth is armed with particularly vicious-looking teeth.

Not infrequently large fishes are the victims of hungry shark attacks. The mighty swordfish, which reaches weights of five hundred pounds and more, is one of those subject to foraging sharks. The mako, especially, is a deadly enemy of the swordfish.

An encounter between those two species was witnessed by a group of sport-fishermen off Rhode Island a few years ago. The swordfish, weighing about three hundred pounds, was at the sea's surface, taking his ease in the sun-warmed water. What he did not know was that a large mako was coming up behind him. The swordfish could not see the shark because the mako was directly in back of him, a blind spot in the swordfish's vision. Swiftly the attacker moved in and instantly bit off the swordfish's tail. Now the big gamefish was without his "propeller" and helpless to escape. Methodically the mako proceeded to remove his victim from the scene, biting and tearing off great mouthfuls that could have weighed as much as thirty to fifty pounds each. Within minutes it was all over, with only a red stain in the sea to mark where the one-sided encounter had taken place.

Since most sharks have the same general form and set of fins, it can be difficult to distinguish among them, especially when seen in the water. However, there are certain details which aid in their identification. Size of course is one. Color can be a

Two makos are suspended from the ginpole and a third hangs from the rail of the 42-foot Cricket II as she drifts on the ocean to try for others

Frank T. Moss

help too when fishes are still in the water and close enough to the surface to be seen. Sometimes the fins are darker on their tips or edges and provide clues for identification. For the experienced observer, certain of the fins, their sizes and positioning, determine the species. The long pectoral fins of the blue shark are an example. Some sharks can be identified by the fact of a noticeably larger or smaller first dorsal fin, or perhaps the shape of the tail.

In most cases though, it is a combination of such details as those just mentioned, rather than any one or two of them alone, that produce the identification.

If there is a single detail that can lead to positive identification of a shark it is the teeth. In many instances they are so distinctive as to be the only clue needed to establish identification.

Above: A five-foot smooth hammerhead on board the research vessel *Dolphin* in July, 1967. The tag on the dorsal fin is used by scientists to keep track of a fish's movements.

Right: Close up of same specimen's head. Eyes are located at outer tips of head.

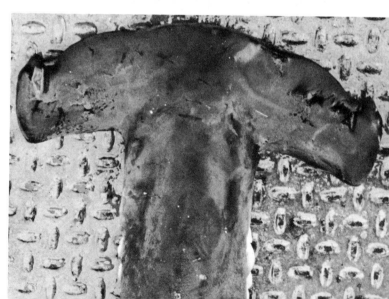

This means of confirming identity has been employed in instances where sharks have attacked small boats, actually biting them and losing a few teeth in the vessels' planks in the process. On some occasions of attacks on humans, sharks' teeth have broken off in a wound.

The teeth of some sharks, such as the white or maneater, are shaped like broad triangles. Others, like those of the porbeagle, have a high middle section with a lesser point on either side, while the mako's teeth are tall, narrow, curving triangles. The distinct notch in the rear margin of the teeth of the tiger shark distinguishes him from all others.

Among the many kinds of sharks, the vast majority of species assume the typical and distinctive profile of their breed. Whatever the species and the variations among them, most sharks share certain basic characteristics. The "standard" shark body form has a typical first dorsal fin, a snout that is slender when viewed in profile, a tail quite unlike that of any other fish, and heads that are reasonably similar in appearance. But there are also some curious deviations from this general "blueprint" for shark construction.

One of the best known is the hammerhead, so called because of the shape of his head. Viewed from above, the head resembles a hammer with the eyes located on each end. Biologists have theorized that the broad head may aid this unusual creature in navigating and securing food. However, no one knows how or why the head developed in that strange fashion. There are several species of hammerheads throughout the world, and they all share that weird-looking head plus a bad reputation.

Lesser known than the hammerheads are thresher sharks, and they are unusual in quite another way. Threshers are distinctive because of the tremendously elongated upper lobe of their tails. This portion of the tail is so long that it just about equals the length of the creature's body. In other words, on a sixteen-foot thresher, eight feet of that length would be tail.

It is this long lobe of his tail and the way he uses it that give the thresher his name. He literally wields it like a scythe to group fishes in a tight circle for a meal. It is a powerful tail, and with it he can stun and kill his prey.

One of the most unusual members of the family is the angel shark, found in many waters of the world. Here we see a radical departure from the usual shark form. With his squat, disk-like body, this creature looks more like his distant relatives the skates and rays than he does the members of his own family. From his appearance one would gather that the angel shark is a kind of in-between form that has come down to us millions of years after the sharks, rays, and skates branched off from common ancestors and went their separate ways. It would seem the angel shark never could make up his mind what he wanted to be, a ray or a shark. Meanwhile, scientists decided for him because of his sharp teeth and the fact that his gill slits are partly on the side of his body.

The following chart of sharks mentioned in this book is only a sampling of the many species found throughout the world. The sharks are listed in order of decreasing sizes based on known or reported maximums, followed by general distribution.

This common thresher is 12.5 feet long, more than half of it tail. Discovered at a beach in Rhode Island in August, 1967, it was shot as a safety precaution and, still active, was landed by the lifeguard with a gaff.

David D. Chestnut

Whale shark	Reported to 60 feet	Tropical belts of all oceans
Basking shark	To 40 and 50 feet	Temperate and boreal waters of the North and South Atlantic, as well as North and South Pacific
White shark	To 36 feet	Widespread in tropical, subtropical, and warm-temperate zones of all oceans
Tiger shark	To 30 feet	Worldwide in tropical and subtropical seas; along northern coast during warmer months
Thresher shark	To 20 feet	Warm temperate and subtropical latitudes
Blue shark	Reported to 15 and 20 feet	Worldwide in tropical and temperate seas; along northeastern United States in warmer months
Great hammerhead shark	To 15 feet	Possibly worldwide in tropical and subtropical seas
Nurse shark	To 14 feet	Both sides of the tropical and subtropical Atlantic; common in Caribbean and near southern Florida; Gulf of California to Panama and Ecuador
Bronze whaler shark	To 14 feet	Australia and New Zealand

Dusky shark	Reported to 14 feet	Warm temperate and tropical regions on both sides of Atlantic; common along east coast of United States
Whitetip shark	To 12 and 13 feet	Tropical and subtropical Atlantic; Mediterranean
Mako shark	To 12 feet	Tropical and warm temperate Atlantic
Black whaler shark	To 12 feet	Australia and New Zealand
Porbeagle shark	Reported to 12 feet	North Atlantic; North Pacific; Australia and New Zealand
Bull shark (also cub shark)	To 12 feet	General distribution in the western Atlantic Ocean
Lemon shark	To 11 feet	Western Atlantic from Brazil to North Carolina; tropical waters off Western Africa
Sand shark (also sand tiger shark)	To 10 feet	Along eastern coast of United States to southern Brazil; Mediterranean; western and southern Africa
Gray nurse shark	To 10 feet	Australia
Zambezi shark	To 8 feet	Eastern and southern coast of South Africa; Zambezi River; other rivers along those seaboards

Large blacktip shark (also spinner shark)	To 8 feet	Tropical and subtropical western Atlantic; both coasts of Florida; Puerto Rico and Cuba
Lake Nicaragua shark	To 8 feet	Only in Lake Nicaragua and its tributaries
Ganges shark	To 7 feet	Indian Ocean and Ganges River
Angel shark (American species)	To 4 and 5 feet	Eastern coast of United States to West Indies; northern reaches of the Gulf of Mexico
Smooth dogfish	To 4 feet	Eastern coast of United States to Uruguay and Brazil

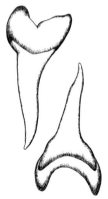

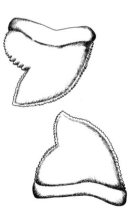

Distinctive shark teeth, uppers and lowers of (from left to right) the mako, the white or maneater, and the tiger

Jan Cook

4. Shark Attacks

Generations of mariners and coastal peoples have feared sharks. It is easy to understand why. Many a shipwrecked sailor has seen a shipmate vanish suddenly under the waves, with only an ugly blotch of red on the tide to tell of his fate. Coastal peoples around the world have heard the anguished scream of a friend or neighbor as a shark struck in shallow water. It was of little interest to the survivors what kind of shark did the attacking. They only knew it was a shark. And so it came to be that all sharks were labeled as dangerous villains, an accusation that many people still believe to this day.

In 1958, a Shark Research Panel of experts from several countries was organized to begin a worldwide program of shark study. Dr. Perry W. Gilbert, professor of Zoology at Cornell University, Ithaca, New York, is chairman of the group, which is sponsored by the American Institute of Biological Sciences and supported by funds from the Office of Naval Research. By studying the behavior and biology of

Dr. Perry W. Gilbert in his study at Cornell University, Ithaca, New York

Barrett Gallagher

sharks, the panel hopes to find a solution to the shark attack problem.

The first scientific record of shark attacks throughout the world was compiled by the Research Panel in 1959—thirty-six unprovoked and three provoked attacks, of which about one-third were fatal.

Of the 250 species of sharks that have been identified so far, about two dozen are known to attack man.

In one of the worst shark villainies ever to occur in the United States the assassin was proved to be a white shark.

A series of five attacks occurred during the summer of 1916 along the New Jersey seacoast. All took place within eleven panicky days, and all were blamed on the same cruising maneater. Four of the victims died and the fifth was severely injured.

The assaults began on July 2 when a 24-year-old man was attacked while swimming in only five feet of water at Beach Haven, New Jersey. He died in a hospital. Four days later and thirty-five miles away, another man was killed by a shark at Spring Lake, New Jersey. On July 12, a boy and a man swimming in Matawan Creek at Sandy Hook, New Jersey, were torn apart by a shark. Another boy in the same general disaster area was bitten and slashed between hips and knees, but recovered.

An intensive hunt for the killer was launched by men armed with rifles, harpoons, and nets. Two days after the last attack, an 8½-foot white shark was captured off South Amboy, New Jersey. In the monster's stomach was a quantity of flesh and bones. After this capture the attacks promptly ceased, and there was little doubt but that the white shark had been the terror.

Another trait that makes white sharks particularly dangerous is their aggressiveness. They have been known to charge boats on occasion. Shark-fishing expert Captain Mundus has had maneaters surface and seize the transom of his boat the *Cricket II* in their jaws. He also has had them bite the boat's bottom, breaking off their teeth in her planks, which he finds when the boat comes out of the water for overhaul. The boat's bottom planking is two inches thick, and sometimes the teeth are in to a depth of one inch. "You can imagine," says Captain Mundus, "what would happen if a big maneater were to bite into thinner planking and shake his head a couple of times. He could tear a good-size hole in the boat."

There are several recorded instances of white sharks attacking boats. On one occasion reported by the National Geographic Society for Nova Scotia waters, a large

97517

Right: The Zambezi shark is particularly menacing because of its habit of going into rivers in search of prey

Oceonographic Research Institute, Durban, Union of South Africa

Below: This whaler shark is about to be killed for research. The spear-fisherman is ready to use a hypodermic spear-gun filled with fast-acting poison.

Australian News and Information Bureau

white shark attacked a dory containing two men. Such was the speed and force of the assault that a hole was stove in the craft and she sank. One of the occupants was drowned. Apparently the attacker did not bother either man. Perhaps he was dazed from having hit the boat with such force.

Another proven killer is the Zambezi shark of South Africa and Mozambique. The late Dr. David Davies, South Africa's noted authority on sharks, considered the Zambezi an even more dangerous killer than the white shark or blue pointer, as the white is called in his country. The Zambezi shark is particularly menacing because of its habit of coming into rivers.

Several mutilating and fatal attacks have been blamed on this killer along the coast of South Africa's Province of Natal on the Indian Ocean. In one case a man was

Impressive girth and length give considerable weight to white sharks. A sixteen- to seventeen-foot maneater such as this can weigh well over a ton.

Captain Frank Mundus

wading across a stream with his son on his shoulders. At midstream a Zambezi made a passing swipe at the man, slashing him. This knocked the man off balance and the boy tumbled into the water, where he was promptly seized and killed by the shark.

Considerable evidence against hammerheads has accumulated over the years, with attacks on swimmers recorded for British Guiana, Australia, and the United States. In most cases of attack it is not possible to identify the exact species of hammerhead involved.

A hammerhead reportedly killed a man in the Virgin Islands just a few years ago. In another case, this one on Long Island, New York, many years ago, parts of a man were found in a hammerhead when the monster was cut open on the dock. In fairness to the shark, however, it should be stated that finding human fragments in his stomach does not necessarily mean that he killed the man. The man may have been a drowning victim, already quite dead, before the shark got to him.

Nonfatal attacks on swimmers by hammerheads have been reported from California and Florida. One instance in the latter state was noted by Dr. Edward Gudger, curator emeritus of fishes of the American Museum of Natural History. In that incident a hammerhead, described as about eight feet long, zeroed in on a young woman swimming two hundred feet from shore at West Palm Beach. The victim received severe lacerations of one thigh and calf, but was rescued by a lifeguard, and fortunately recovered. In another nonfatal Florida attack a man was bitten by a hammerhead when his boat capsized off Fort Lauderdale.

Another vicious species of shark is the tiger. Among several Australian attacks blamed on tigers is a case mentioned by Dr. Perry Gilbert. On the same day off New South Wales, a shark killed two men. Next day an eleven-foot, nine-inch tiger was caught, and in his stomach was one of the victim's hands, identified by a peculiar scar. Dr. Gilbert also reports two grisly Florida incidents. A fourteen-foot tiger captured off Miami Beach yielded the dismembered body of a victim identified as C. K. Ormund, Jr. That same year, 1943, an eleven-foot tiger caught near Boca Grande on Florida's western coast contained the remains of an unidentified man. In both cases, however, it was never established whether or not the victims were already dead when devoured by the predators.

Like white sharks, the larger tigers can be doubly dangerous because of their unpredictable attacks on small boats. Sometimes the assaults are provoked, as in an episode described by Dr. Gudger in which an 11½-footer attacked a boat after being harpooned off Key West, Florida. Sometimes the attacks are unprovoked. Such was the case in another Florida incident, this one off Miami. A man was following a fourteen-foot tiger in his boat when the monster suddenly turned and charged the craft with such viciousness that a one-foot section of its fiberglass and wood hull was torn away.

The more man learns about sharks, the more the list of proven killers seems to lengthen. Names of known man-eaters in the waters off Australia are the gray nurse, the tiger shark, and members of a group known as whaler sharks. It is said that in Australian waters whaler sharks are chiefly responsible for attacks in harbors, while tigers are the villains along seacoast beaches.

The Lake Nicaragua shark
of Central America infests
the fresh water lake of the
same name.

No list of known killers would be complete without mention of the Lake Nicaragua shark of Central America and the Ganges shark of India. Both of these killers are especially interesting because they inhabit fresh water.

Lake Nicaragua at one time was a bay of the Pacific Ocean but was closed off apparently through volcanic action which created an isthmus. Gradually, as the water in the lake became fresh, the sharks trapped there adapted to the new conditions. They are much dreaded by Nicaraguans living around the lake. Several fatalities, along with mutilating assaults which have cost victims arms and legs, have been attributed to the vicious predators. The Ganges shark, equally ferocious, is believed responsible for maiming and fatal attacks on Indians making religious pilgrimages to the river.

In addition to the known killers, there are several species of the larger sharks that should be regarded as dangerous. Although attacks are unproven, the heavily toothed blue, porbeagle, whitetip, and mako are viewed with suspicion. Dr. Gilbert notes unauthenticated instances of attacks, or at least threatening movements by blues in California, Japan, Australia, and New Jersey. While making an underwater motion picture off Montauk, New York, famed underwater naturalist Peter Gimbel had a blue shark make three distinct "passes" at him, fortunately without injury.

The list of potentially dangerous sharks goes on to include many species throughout the world. For United States waters, in addition to those already mentioned, Dr. Gilbert lists the large blacktip, lemon, bull, and dusky. The nurse shark, not to be confused with the dreaded gray nurse of Australia, and the sand shark generally are

considered harmless by fishermen, and that may be true so far as aggression is concerned. However, both species are on record as biting when molested. The nurse shark is easily identified by a fleshy barbel on the edge of each nostril which gives the appearance of small tusks or teeth.

The fact is, sharks of any species, especially the larger, more active ones, should be considered dangerous. This does not mean that they will go out of their way to attack humans. It does mean, however, that any familiarity with them is to be discouraged. Even so-called harmless sharks can be dangerous when annoyed, injured, or handled carelessly.

Any shark should be looked upon as an unpredictable wild animal, each with its own behavior pattern. It must be remembered, too, that a shark's reactions will vary from day to day. Thus a shark that will be attracted to a swimmer out of curiosity one moment may be frightened away the next, or vice versa. And what begins as an approach out of simple inquisitiveness could change in an instant to an aggressive attack.

Much is to be learned about the patterns of shark attacks. It is known that bright, shiny things and objects with contrasting colors tend to attract them. Blood in the water is a positive attraction. Swimmers who have scraped themselves on coral or rocks can lure sharks. Skindivers sometimes court disaster by attaching fish they have speared to their belts. Any blood from the fish can draw sharks. The visitors may be harmless, but if they go for the bleeding fish at a skindiver's waist they can very easily bite the diver instead.

This view of a nurse shark shows the distinctive barbels resembling tusks at the nostrils

New York Zoological Society Photo

Because so little is known about the patterns of shark attacks and the influences of variables such as water temperature and other factors, it is impossible to state a positive defense for any swimmer approached by a shark. Making a commotion in the water might repel a timid shark, or attract a more aggressive one. Similarly, swimmers have reported that punching a shark in the nose will drive him away. That has worked in some instances. In others the marauder has circled and attacked again. Authorities vary in their advice to swimmers on an intelligent approach to the shark problem; nevertheless, the consensus seems to be the advisability of caution and calmness. Be cautious where you swim—refrain from swimming in waters known or suspected of containing sharks. If you should find yourself in the water with one leave as quickly as possible but *calmly*, as any panicky thrashing is likely to excite a shark.

Considering the astronomical numbers of sharks at large in the world's seas, attacks on humans are quite infrequent. In some locales, however, attacks have been more concentrated than in others. The Australian coast near Sydney is an example. Another is the Natal shore of South Africa, notably in the vicinity of Durban. Concentrations of attacks also were recorded during World War II by fliers downed at sea and the survivors of torpedoings.

Accordingly, in recent years efforts have been intensified to find ways to protect bathers and others in shark-infested waters.

Different types of "shark-proof" fences have been tried to protect swimmers. One of these consisted of a curtain of bubbles, constantly moving upward from pipes in the water. This successfully screened out some species of sharks but others swam through it quite unconcernedly.

Shark lookout stations have been established at many Australian beaches to warn of the presence of sharks

Australian News and Information Bureau

Right: This Navy shark deterrent consisting of a black plasticized bag and orange buoyance rings was designed by Dr. C. Scott Johnson (shown in photo) of the Naval Ordnance Test Station, Point Mugu, California. One advantage of this deterrent is that blood from a wounded man is not released into the ocean.

United States Department of Defense

Various types of wire enclosures for swimmers have been tried also, with varying degrees of success. Most satisfactory of all thus far is an arrangement known as meshing. This consists of stringing a series of metal mesh nets parallel to the beach. The safety record for meshing in South Africa and Australia is most impressive.

61

For the protection of fliers downed at sea and survivors of ship sinkings, scientists have been endeavoring to find some sort of substance that would repel sharks in the water. Many kinds of dyes and chemicals have been tested in an effort to find a compound that would either impair a shark's sense of smell or sight, serve as an irritant, or be downright repugnant. Some of the compounds proved effective for certain species, ineffective for others.

Currently a new shark deterrent, designed by Dr. C. Scott Johnson of the Naval Ordnance Test Station, Point Mugu, California, has been undergoing tests. The device consists of a plasticized black bag five feet in length and from two to three feet in diameter. Attached to the top of the bag are three inflatable buoyance rings, colored international orange for visibility. These rings are fitted with mouthpieces, allowing them to be easily inflated by the swimmer. When packed, the bag is carried easily on a life jacket. Once in the water, the swimmer, supported by his life jacket, detaches the bag, fills it with water, crawls inside, and inflates the three rings. One special advantage of this deterrent is that blood and odors from a wounded man which attract sharks are not released into the ocean. Also the bag helps keep its user warm by conserving body heat.

To date no truly universal, sure-fire repellent has been devised, but undoubtedly one will come with more research. Meanwhile, the consoling reminder from Dr. Gilbert is that under ordinary circumstances and when a shark is not provoked the "likelihood of attack is less than that of being struck by lightning." And just a little care and common sense will reduce the chances even further.

5. Sportfishing for Sharks

Many fishermen prefer big, tough, hard-fighting opponents. Sharks meet those requirements nicely. Furthermore, the opportunities for battling sharks are much more numerous than the chances of catching some of the other large game fishes, such as marlins and swordfish. This does not mean that sharks are easier to catch. It is just that there are more of them and, usually, they are located more readily.

The basic sportfishing tackle for sharks is exactly the same as for any other kind of fish; a rod, a reel, and some line. In any kind of fishing, the rod is the primary weapon with which a fish is caught and controlled. It is this item of equipment which takes the shock of the fish's resistance. The line, of course, is the angler's contact with his fish. A reel serves three basic functions. Firstly, it is a convenient means of storing the line, allowing it to run out when the fish runs. Secondly, it has a brake called a drag, which resists the fish in his attempt to escape and helps to tire him. Thirdly, it enables the fisherman to crank his opponent to the boat when the fish tires sufficiently to bring the battle to a conclusion.

Another standard item in angling is what is known as terminal tackle or the rig. Depending upon the kind of fishing being done, the rig can consist of a baited hook or some kind of artificial lure which carries one or more hooks. In the case of the former, the bait impaled on the hook usually is an item of the natural food of the fish being sought. In salt water fishing it may be a piece of clam, a marine worm known as a bloodworm, or even a small fish. The same principle is involved in fishing with an artificial lure. Here the lure is made to resemble some article of food the fish likes. In trout fishing, artificials known as flies are used. There are many different kinds used for these fresh water fish, but generally they are made from feathers and bright-colored bits of other materials to resemble insects on which trout feed. Similarly, there are salt water fishing lures called plugs, squids, jigs, and so on which resemble the food that appeals to larger fishes.

Another important part of the rig in shark fishing is the leader. Leaders are used for various reasons, according to the type of angling done and the fishes sought. In shark fishing they serve a definite purpose, and are of wire for this reason. A shark's hide is so rough that it would rub through ordinary line in a twinkling. Therefore, a wire leader, fifteen to thirty feet long, is inserted in the rig between hook and line.

The major difference between the tackle used for sharks and that employed for any other smaller kinds of fish is that it is heavier and sturdier. It has to be because of the size and enormous strength of some sharks. If you are going to battle a fish weighing from a hundred to five hundred pounds and more you must have suitably strong weapons. The rod must be able to withstand severe bending and great strains as the shark runs, dives, and exerts pull on the line. The reels are proportionately large, not only because they must be strong, but also because they must be able to hold hundreds of yards of fishing line. It is not uncommon for a shark to take two hundred or more yards from a reel during one of his long, fast runs. The line, of course, must be suitably strong also.

Actually, lightweight tackle is sometimes used for sharks. But here, because of the lightness of the equipment, the odds are higher against the angler, with the ever-present threat of broken line or rod. It is because of the greater challenge to their skill that some anglers use light tackle for sharks, but these are usually fishermen who are greatly experienced.

The closing phase of a battle with a good-size blue shark

Captain Frank Mundus

This mako, weighing about 300 pounds, was hooked by an angler whose rod you see in the foreground. The great battler leaped clear of the water in an effort to escape the hook.

Captain Frank Mundus

Sharks can be caught by a variety of sportfishing methods. You can fish in the ocean surf for them, as for smaller species of fishes such as striped bass, bluefish, channel bass, and many others. Or you can fish from an anchored boat, letting your bait sink to varying levels in an effort to locate a cruising shark. Trolling, or the procedure of towing an artificial lure or natural bait behind a boat, will produce sharks occasionally, but it is the least productive of all shark-fishing methods. Unlike certain other game fishes, such as tuna and marlins, sharks do not respond readily to trolled baits and lures.

Surf casting for sharks calls for a particular kind of beach, one that slopes off rapidly into deep water where the sharks can come in to feed. For that reason, and because fighting and landing sharks on an ocean front can be difficult, surf angling for sharks is not a popular method. Also, this type of fishing is not very productive.

However, in Durban, South Africa, surf casting for sharks is perhaps the most popular technique. There the anglers have a long pier that extends well out into the harbor. The sharks are attracted by a shore whaling station nearby. Using very sturdy tackle and large pieces of whale meat as bait, Durban fishermen catch hammerheads, maneaters, gray sharks, and other South African species from the pier. Some of the man-eaters caught there by surf fishing have weighed more than one thousand pounds.

One of the best shark-fishing techniques is that developed by Captain Mundus. The Mundus method, which he has nicknamed "monster fishing," consists of drifting and chumming.

Chumming is an angling procedure in which some item of natural fish food is ladled overboard as a lure

Milt Rosko

Chumming is the process of ladling overboard some kind of natural food that attracts the fish. The chum may be whole shrimp, whole small fishes, pieces of larger fishes, or, very commonly, ground-up pulp. In Captain Mundus' case, he uses either of two kinds of pulp, depending upon the species of shark he is hunting. For most types he ladles a fish pulp overboard. However, for white sharks, the great maneaters, he favors a bloody pulp which he makes by feeding pieces of whale meat through a large electric grinder. Maneaters seem to like this whale meat chum.

Whatever kind of chum is used, the procedure and the objective are the same. In chumming it is important that the food be dropped overboard in an unbroken line. The reason is simple. What occurs is that tidal currents carry the chum away from the boat in a continuous line. Sharks and other fishes smell this food, locate it, and then, as they eat it, come toward the boat where baited hooks are waiting. Should the feeding line be broken, a shark or other fish moving along it toward the boat will come to the break, find no more food, and may then lose interest and swim away.

In shark fishing, chumming's effect is heightened even further by drifting. By letting the boat drift before the wind, with an unbroken stream of chum trailing behind, instead of fishing at anchor, a large amount of sea area can be covered. The chances of contacting wandering sharks therefore is increased considerably.

Among the many sharks available to sportfishermen, one of the most desirable of all is the mako. The mako is a magnificent game fish because he is a fast, stubborn, hard-fighting opponent. He also has a special characteristic, one that most other sharks do not have. Makos can leap clear of the sea in spectacular jumps during the course of a battle with an angler. From his boat, Captain Mundus has seen them jump out of the water to heights of fifteen and sixteen feet as they try to shake the hook from their mouths. In this talent makos often are superior to other game fishes, such as the marlin and sailfish, noted for their leaping ability.

Imagine, then, the power required to send three hundred pounds of fish ten to sixteen feet into the air. Sometimes they will arrow swiftly upward from underneath to attack a bait; and in so doing their momentum carries them right out of the sea. Makos also can accomplish spectacular leaps from a "standing start." This also gives some idea of the power they can exert when fighting rod and reel.

Sometimes the jumps create extra excitement. Not uncommonly a mako will leap when an angler has reeled him in alongside the boat. The big fish may appear to be tired out, but he can summon a surprising amount of reserve power in a last minute effort to escape. When those jumps occur right alongside a boat they can be dangerous as well as exciting. The big danger is that the fish will land right in the boat, and a big, angry mako shark is hardly a pleasant companion in the close quarters of a boat's cockpit.

In at least one instance, a mako actually did land aboard Captain Mundus' *Cricket II* and very nearly caused a tragedy. The angler seemingly had conquered his mako after a long, hard fight and had reeled the brute right next to the boat. Perhaps sensing that the battle for freedom was just about over, the mako summoned a reserve of strength and burst clear of the sea, headed for the sky like a rocket. When he came down he landed on board in a seat that had been occupied only seconds

This lemon shark is the type of big, tough, hard-fighting opponent with which many fishermen like to do battle

Marineland of Florida

before by the boat's mate. Had the mate been sitting there, he would have been hit on the head with a couple of hundred pounds of mako falling from a height of perhaps ten feet. Luckily for all concerned the shark hit the empty seat and bounced overboard. Minutes later he was captured.

In another incident, reported several years ago, an angler was less fortunate than the mate on the *Cricket II*. In this instance a large mako leaped into the cockpit of a sportfishing boat with such speed and force that his momentum carried him right across the cockpit, then up, over, and out the other side. Along the way he smashed the fighting chair and broke the fisherman's leg.

Not all dramatic experiences in shark fishing are confined to the mako. One time a large maneater, estimated at one thousand pounds, had been attracted to a boat by chum, but he refused to take any of the three baits that were offered to him. Instead, the white shark swam leisurely around the boat. The mate stood in a corner of the cockpit watching him. Suddenly the huge beast thrust his head out of the water, opening his jaws which exposed his frightening teeth. The mate opened his mouth to call to the captain, but was so awed by the sight of the shark that he could not make a sound. The maneater then moved near where the mate was standing and seized the boat in his teeth. He held on for a few minutes while the dumbfounded mate watched. Finally, the big shark released his grip and sank back into the sea.

Some of the most exciting shark fishing occurs at night. The darkness out on the lonely ocean, the sea's inky blackness, and not being able to see one's opponent all combine to provide a very special kind of mystery and suspense. There is a practical aspect of night shark fishing also, for the fish feed more actively during the hours of darkness than in the daytime. Catches, therefore, can be better.

One night that never will be forgotten occurred several years ago about fifteen or twenty miles off Montauk, New York. Except for occasional waves of silver light as the moon peeped from scudding clouds, the night was dark. The ocean was like a sea of jet black ink, and the only sounds were the soft slapping of the waves as the boat drifted with the breeze.

A chum line had been established, and the anglers had their baits down in the water waiting for any shark that might be attracted to the boat. An hour or more passed without any sign of action. Then suddenly, the fishermen heard a strange slurping noise off in the darkness. All of them had fished for sharks at night many times before, but never had they heard a sound such as this. No one could identify it. In the pitch darkness the anglers could see nothing. The fishermen felt their hair begin to rise as the eerie sound drew closer and louder. What kind of thing was out there making that noise as it came toward their boat in the night?

Then someone remembered a lantern. Lighting it, the men discovered the source of the weird sound. It was a large shark, moving along the chum line at the surface, sucking in pieces of the fish chum.

Much of the excitement of night fishing for sharks is the suspense in being unable to see the monster, or to identify it or gauge its size. From the moment some unseen creature seizes the bait and takes yards and yards of line off the reel as it races away in the dark, the suspense does not lessen until the very last, when by the light of a lantern, the beast is hauled out of the sea.

Often the greatest danger in shark fishing occurs after the capture is complete. Sharks do not die easily. Unless they have been killed with a rifle or shotgun, they can remain alive out of water for a surprising length of time, even in a hot sun. Many boats are equipped with a ginpole, a simple vertical structure, from which sharks are hung head down. Pulleys effect the lifting of the shark out of the water, tail first. Danger is ever present while the shark is hanging from the ginpole. Even a seemingly dead shark that has been hanging motionless for an hour or more can suddenly "come to life," turn quickly, and snap its jaws at anyone standing nearby.

An experienced shark fisherman never brings a live shark of any kind into a boat. More than once a presumably "dead" shark has suddenly sprung into action, ready and able to seize anything or anybody within reach.

Because sharks are so tenacious of life, some anglers endeavor to kill them right after catching. The surest way to accomplish this is with a high-powered rifle or a shotgun blast at short range. Either way the shot must hit the brain or sever the spinal cord to be effective. Many fishermen try to dispatch their sharks by towing them backward behind the boat. This forces water through the gills at a rapid rate and, theoretically at least, drowns the fish. This must be done for several minutes at a lively pace, and the method is not always effective.

Some anglers try to club the shark to death right after catching by hitting it repeatedly on the head with a baseball bat or similar object. This method is not dependable either. It can merely stun the shark temporarily, leading to a belief that it is dead.

Later that "dead" shark can come to life very suddenly. Another danger in clubbing sharks is that the angler might be using an instrument that is too short and miss. In that case the still-alive shark could bite the clubber's arm as it went by its head. Even if the monster's teeth only grazed the arm they are so sharp they could cause deep and very painful lacerations.

Careless handling on the dock by spectators and inexperienced fishermen also can lead to trouble. Sharks hanging by their tails from a weighing device or merely lying on a dock seem to extend an invitation to examine them, but to poke, inspect, or handle a shark that has any spark of life left is to risk injury.

Even experienced fishermen are fooled by seemingly dead sharks sometimes. We know of a case in which a seasoned shark hunter was about to weigh a 300-pounder he had caught several hours earlier. The shark made no move when a rope was put around its tail and it was hoisted up on the scale. The angler had climbed a ladder alongside the scale to read the dial. Just as the shark was lifted alongside him, the creature suddenly began threshing wildly and attempting to bite. That shark literally chased the man to the top of the ladder.

Captain Mundus recommends a test that is quite accurate in determining when a shark is dead. Using a pole that enables you to stand clear of the fish, nudge it in one of the eyes. If it does not move, or if the eye itself does not move, that shark is dead. Even if only its eyeball moves after touching, some life remains and caution is the word. Sharks can be handled without any difficulty when they are dead, just as long as touching the mouth and jaws is avoided.

6. The Shark in Legend and Sea Lore

When man fears a creature, or is awed by it, or admires it even though he is afraid of it, he often creates stories about that creature. Many of these myths sound strange to us today. We may find them difficult or utterly impossible to believe, or we may even laugh at them. However, it should be remembered that such tales took root in the dark ages of man's knowledge. Often he created them to explain things he did not understand. Frequently they were handed down in folklore, to be believed for generations afterward. Many such legends, contrary to knowledge, persist even to this day among primitive people. For ages man's "knowledge" of sharks was composed largely of a mixture of fact, fancy, legends, and folk tales.

The word "shark" is old in the English language. The *Oxford Universal Dictionary* traces it back to 1569. But no one seems to know exactly where it came from. Many years ago it was suggested that it stemmed from an old German word, *schurke*, meaning "villain," and that English sailors picked it up in their travels and eventually

changed it to its present form. That too is uncertain, but at least it is in harmony with the shark's evil reputation.

In the absence of writings we can only imagine what primitive man thought about sharks. It seems safe to assume that he was scared of them, probably fearing them just as he did the land monsters around him.

Later, when ancient civilizations began noting their impressions of life about them in writings, drawings, statuary, and so forth, there came some of the earliest recordings of sharks. Archaeologists have unearthed Indian pottery in South America that bears crude images of sharks, while surgical implements made of shark teeth were found in the Ellice Islands of the Pacific.

In ancient Japanese mythology there was a god of storms whose name translated as Shark Man. It has been said that the Chinese knew of the terror sharks struck in the hearts of Japanese. Eventually they capitalized on it when, during World War II, they painted the vicious open mouth of a shark with its teeth prominently displayed on the front section of their war planes. An American squadron under General Claire Chennault flying those planes against the Nipponese came to be called the Flying Tigers. This name was derived from the tiger shark.

Sharks figure prominently in the lore and legends of South Pacific Ocean island peoples. To some of the primitive islanders sharks were demons to be avoided at all costs. To others they were gods. Among some South Pacific peoples the belief was that the shark gods had to be appeased by human sacrifices. Men, women, and children were tossed to the beasts. Among the Maoris of New Zealand and in the Fiji

A Flying Tiger plane and pilot from the American fighter
squadron of World War II

U.S. Air Force Photo

Islands sharks had been worshipped as deities for longer than the oldest inhabitants could recall. Not always were the fish considered evil gods. The Maoris, for example, looked upon sharks as symbols of good fortune and even incorporated the hammerhead in the design of the rafters of their huts.

In the South Pacific islands many religious beliefs developed around sharks. In some of these, men took the form of sharks after death. In others the procedure was reversed, and the sharks came ashore in human form, often to do mischief. In the Solomon Islands there was a belief that dead relatives were reincarnated as good sharks. The bad sharks were those that were not relatives.

In ancient Hawaii there was a strong belief that sharks could assume human form and come ashore, perhaps to perform evil deeds. The Hawaiians called these creatures *mano kanaka* (shark men). Apparently, later islanders made human sacrifices to sharks also. In the 1800's, Russian explorer Otto von Katzebue reported seeing a large pen, about where Pearl Harbor now stands, into which men, women, and children were tossed, to be torn apart by captive sharks. Even in comparatively recent times there were coral altars in the Solomon Islands for sacrifices to sharks. The victims were strangled on the altars, after which the bodies were dropped into the sea to waiting sharks.

Human sacrifices to the monsters have been recorded in many parts of the world. Certain tribes on the western coast of Africa worshipped sharks as gods. Mostly their offerings to the sea deities were chickens and domestic animals, but at least once a year a child was tied to a stake in shallow water at low tide, to be left to the

Left: Surgical implements of shark teeth from Vaitupu, Ellice Islands, look more like weapons

American Museum of Natural History

Below: This is a Maori rafter pattern design of the hammerhead shark known as the mangopare

*Dominion Museum,
Wellington, New Zealand*

appetite of prowling man-eaters. One of the strangest of such customs was practiced in India long ago. The followers of an unusual religious cult made a yearly pilgrimage to the sea, and there on the shore voluntarily offered themselves as sacrifices. Wading into water infested with sharks, they were bitten, torn apart, and dragged beneath the surface. It is said that wave after wave of these pilgrims walked into the sea until it turned red with blood.

The famous painting "Gulf Stream" by Winslow Homer (1899) shows a man, adrift in an unmasted boat, threatened by a waterspout and sharks

The Metropolitan Museum of Art, Wolfe Fund, 1906

Legends of men taking the form of sharks after death are not confined to South Pacific Isles. In Irish folklore there is a tale about a man who underwent such a change. According to the story, the man had done evil things in his life, and after death he was reincarnated as a shark, his punishment being to cruise the waters of the southern Irish coast for seven years. It was part of the legend that this particular shark always appeared off the beach just before a bad storm.

Mariners of the great era of sailing ships were largely a highly superstitious lot, and sharks literally swam through the countless stories told in waterfront taverns and by lamplight in the forecastle crew's quarters on long voyages. Invariably sharks were evil rogues in those tales.

Much of the fear and awe in which sharks are viewed by sailors is dramatized by the painting "Gulf Stream" by the noted American seascape artist Winslow Homer. In "Gulf Stream," we see a lone mariner cast adrift on the vast, rolling expanse of an ocean. His small sailing craft has been dismasted, and without sails she drifts helplessly at the whims of wind and current. As if the predicament were not bad enough, circling the craft and plainly visible are large sharks, waiting for the sailor to fall into the sea.

It is not uncommon, even today, for sharks to collect in the wake of an ocean-going vessel when garbage is tossed overboard. In the days of sailing ships, any congregating of sharks, even if attracted by garbage, was looked upon with a certain amount of dread. To those old-timers, sharks could not mean anything but evil. The fact that the gray sea wolves occasionally bit off the propeller-like device trailed astern to indicate the ship's speed did nothing to change that feeling.

On long voyages sailors who died aboard ship were buried at sea. It became a persistent superstition that when a shark appeared in the wake of a vessel it was a bad omen, meaning that someone was going to die. You can be sure that many a sailor, home from a long voyage, told about how sharks suddenly appeared around his vessel and, sure enough, soon afterward a shipmate fell from the rigging or died from some ailment.

Mariner's stories often told about individual sharks that prowled a particular area or port and became so well known they were given names. Usually they were large monsters with especially sinister reputations. One whose name came up in forecastle lore or wherever sailing men swapped yarns about sharks was Shanghai Bill. Why he was called "Shanghai" is not explained, but it seems strange in light of the fact that old Bill prowled the waters of a harbor in Barbados in the West Indies. Then there was Port Royal Jack, species unidentified but possibly a tiger or white shark, that frequented the harbor at Kingston, Jamaica, also in the West Indies.

Recently, and not part of an old salt's tale, there is Barnacle Lil, the enormous white shark that defied the angling skills of famous big game fisherman Alf Dean in the waters of the Great Australian Bight. Barnacle Lil's length was estimated at a good twenty feet, and her weight would have been in thousands of pounds. She was recognizable by her huge bulk and a peculiar scar on one of her gill covers.

Alf Dean had two memorable angling encounters with Barnacle Lil. In the first he fought the enormous maneater for an hour and a half and finally had to cut the line to keep from being pulled overboard when his reel jammed. In the second battle, a fierce fight lasting about five hours, Alf's fingers stiffened in fatigue, blisters developed on his hands, and his arms ached with the strain. Three times he brought Lil close to his boat, and each time at the last minute she swam away with such force that twenty men could not have stopped her. Finally, Alf's wire leader snapped from rubbing on the boat's rail, tearing out a section of the rail and allowing the giant shark to escape to become a living legend.

All the superstitions and stories of evil doings spun by oldtime sailing men have not prevented ships from being named after sharks. More than one United States Navy vessel has carried the name *Shark*. The first was a 198-ton warship, a schooner mounting twelve guns and captained by Lieutenant Matthew C. Perry. The *Shark* was the young naval officer's first command. Later, as Commodore Perry, he was to take his place in American history by leading an expedition to open Japanese ports to the western world.

Since then, several United States Navy ships have borne the word shark in one variation or another. The majority of them have been submarines, following the Navy's practice of naming these undersea boats after fishes. Four of the submarines named for sharks met tragic ends. Two of them disappeared while on patrol duty in World War II. Two more, the *Squalus*, a generic name for various species of sharks, sank off Portsmouth, New Hampshire, in 1939; while the *Thresher* was lost with all hands on a test dive in 1963, east of Boston. Both submarines were on routine operations.

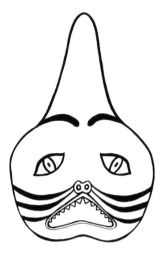

A typical representation of a shark among the Northwest Coast Indians. A high, tapered forehead, a mouth curved downward and filled with pointed teeth, and a series of lines on each cheek representing the gill slits are the characteristic symbols of the shark.

Jan Cook

However great the aura of dread, superstition, and evil that has followed sharks down through the ages, it has not stopped man from making references to them in many ways. Because of their sinister reputation, the word shark has assumed some unpleasant meanings in speaking about humans. For instance, there is the term "loan shark," applied to anyone who preys upon people who desperately need money by lending it to them at illegally high rates of interest. Then there is the "card shark," a professional gambler whose honesty may be questionable. In general, a human shark is anyone who preys upon his fellow man for one reason or another.

The Tlingit Indians of Alaska and British Columbia divided their tribes into subdivisions known as "shark lodges." Apparently, knowledge of sharks spread far and wide among American Indians. Certain tribes living far from the sea were known to nickname rattlesnakes "little sharks of the woods." Totems and other tribal emblems have varied figures representing sharks, probably a kind of tribute to those fearsome creatures.

Sharks have been immortalized in literature by Mark Twain in an episode titled "Cecil Rhodes and the Shark," which appeared in the book *Following the Equator*. The short story is fanciful and humorous but its central character is not. Cecil John Rhodes, an Englishman, went to South Africa in 1870, where he subsequently amassed a vast fortune from the famous Kimberley diamond fields. In Mark Twain's short story, Cecil Rhodes, then a penniless young man visiting Sydney, Australia, happened to catch a nineteen-foot shark that had swallowed a newspaper published in London ten days earlier. The newspaper, Rhodes discovered, carried news about the wool market. There being no fast means of communication between England and Australia, Rhodes was able to use the advance information about the wool market to make a large fortune. Or so wrote Mark Twain, presumably with tongue in cheek.

Probably, the greatest work of literature involving the shark is Ernest Hemingway's *The Old Man and the Sea*. This short novel won the 1953 Pulitzer Prize for fiction and was cited in the 1954 Nobel Prize for literature which was awarded to Mr. Hemingway.

In this story Hemingway tells the tragic tale of a Cuban fisherman in the Gulf Stream who catches a huge marlin only to have it literally stripped to a skeleton by sharks. The story is exciting reading as we see the wiles of the "Old Man" pitted against nature, the sea, and the sea's most feared animal, the shark.

7. The Shark as an Aid to Man

The sharks' greatest contribution to man has been in the products that have been derived from these animals' bodies. One of the oldest-known of these products is shark skin. The hide, removed from the shark and with the dermal denticles left in it, is called shagreen. Back in the days of great sailing ships, shagreen was used to smooth wooden surfaces and in other chores for which we would employ sandpaper today.

Another long-known shark product is leather. It is the strongest leather known, with a tensile strength up to about 7,000 pounds, or three and a half tons, per square inch. That is to say, to pull a piece of that shark leather apart you would have to hang a weight of at least 7,000 pounds to the square inch on it. Closest in strength is good cowhide, which has a tensile strength of about 5,000 pounds per square inch.

Shark leather also is the most durable kind known. For that reason it is excellent for wallets, belts, shoes, pocketbooks, and similar items subjected to much use. Articles made from shark skin will wear almost indefinitely. The late Captain William E. Young, a retired commercial fisherman and lifelong student of fishes, had a belt he had been wearing for fifteen years, and from the looks of it the belt was good for another fifteen years, if not more.

The dermal denticles usually are removed when shark skin is processed into leather. But many years ago an unidentified gentleman came up with a clever use for shagreen. He invented a pickpocket-proof wallet. This wallet was made from shark skin with the dermal denticles left in for a definite purpose. When its owner put the wallet in his pocket he inserted it "with the grain," so to speak. In other words, the dermal denticles were pushed down out of the way and the wallet slid in smoothly. When a thief tried to remove the wallet, the pocket's lining rubbed against the dermal denticles and pulled them up. Hundreds of tiny "thorns" engaged the pocket's lining, and the wallet was held fast.

Sometimes, shark hides are processed in such a way that the denticles are left in, but their points are smoothed off. The resulting modified shagreen is fashioned into all sorts of articles, such as fancy inkstands, cases for eyeglasses, and bindings for expensive books.

A sturdy fabric manufactured by textile mills has been given the name sharkskin. Clothing made from this material is extremely durable and long wearing.

Sharks have been the source of several other products in addition to leather. One of them is the rich oil that comes from their oversized livers.

Long ago shark liver oil was burned in lamps like whale oil. In modern times several other industrial uses have been found for it, including tempering steel, making of soaps and cosmetics, as a high grade lubricant, and in the manufacture of paints.

It also has proved to be of value in the pharmaceutical field. For years the principal source of Vitamin A was cod liver oil, used to fortify the diets of humans, animals, and poultry. Many a boy and girl had to gulp down tablespoonfuls of vile-tasting "tonics" containing cod liver oil. Much of the cod liver oil used in these compounds was imported, notably from Norway. Then during World War II, with Norway occupied by the Nazis, that supply was cut off. A search was begun for a new source of vitamin A.

Eventually, the search turned to shark livers. Scientists reasoned that sharks' oil-rich livers might contain vitamin A. They were correct and the hunt was on. The experiments revealed that the liver oil of some species is amazingly rich in vitamin A. That from the small, common shark known as the dogfish was found to have ten times more vitamin A than cod liver oil. Analysis showed that liver oil from certain other sharks contained as much as a hundred times more.

So, just prior to the United States' entry into World War II, was born a specialized American commercial fishery, one in which thousands of sharks were captured for their valuable livers. As an illustration, at a contemporary California fishery prices paid for sharks zoomed to astonishing heights. Before the war, shark carcasses there brought about ten dollars per ton; and that was paid mainly because sharks were destructive of fishermen's nets, as well as beause they could be ground up for fertilizer. With a rapidly increasing demand for shark liver oil, the price doubled and quadrupled, climbed swiftly to $100 a ton, then skyrocketed to $1,200 a ton. During the war the price soared to $1,500 a ton. Soupfin shark, the liver oil of which was found to contain as much as a hundred times more vitamin A than cod liver oil, were especially valuable, bringing up to $2,000 per ton.

The World War II shark-liver boom made many commercial fishermen quite wealthy. How the industry mushroomed is indicated by reports of their earnings. One is said to have caught $17,500-worth of soupfin shark in four days, while another grossed $40,000 in five months. Happily for the sharks and unfortunately for the fishermen, this prosperity was not to last. In time, pharmaceutical chemistry was to discover ways to produce vitamins synthetically and more cheaply.

No list of industrial applications of sharks would be complete without mention of the uses of shark meal. This material is made by drying shark flesh and pulverizing it. The resulting meal has been helpful in agriculture as a food-fortifier for farm animals and poultry. Further, since shark flesh is rich in nitrogen, the meal also is a good fertilizer.

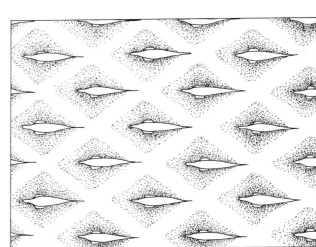

Enlarged drawing of sharkskin, showing dermal denticles. When these sharp protuberances are removed, a beautifully grained leather results.

Jan Cook

In the Orient, one of the very oldest uses of sharks was as food for human consumption. People in China, Japan, and Korea have been eating sharks for generations. An ancient delicacy in China is a rather thick soup made from shark fins. Even today in places where there are people of Chinese extraction shark fins are sun-dried for later use in making soup. The soupfin shark gets its name because of the soup-making qualities of its fins.

Probably the world's greatest consumers of seafood, the Japanese have been eating shark meat, and they smoke and can quantities of it. Sharks also have entered into the diets in many other parts of the world, including Australia, New Zealand, South American countries, Great Britain, Italy, and other nations of Europe. In parts of England, for example, shark meat is an ingredient of that famous old British dish

Dr. Perry W. Gilbert entering the shark pens at the Lerner Marine Laboratory in an attempt to gain further knowledge of the shark

Dr. Perry W. Gilbert

known as fish and chips; and during World War II Britains found that margarine could be made from shark liver oil.

Today many countries, in addition to those already mentioned, either catch or import thousands of tons of shark meat for food. They include Norway, Mexico, Spain, Denmark, India, Belgium, Ireland and, to a lesser extent, Canada and West Germany. It is interesting to note that in recent years porbeagle sharks have been caught in international waters off the United States' eastern coast for export to European markets, notably Italy.

In the United States and other nations shark meat has not yet gained popular acceptance. Many reasons have been offered in explanation. Some stem from personal tastes in seafoods, and a criticism that shark meat has a strong "fishy" taste. However, it is to be suspected that in many instances there is a matter of superstition or the belief that sharks are scavengers or man-eaters.

That sharks do scavenge occasionally is true; but then, so do many kinds of fishes. It is also true that some sharks living close inshore will devour garbage and carrion when an opportunity arises.

It is most unfortunate that shark meat is not more generally accepted. In the first place, it is nutritious. Secondly, it is high in protein, more so than other food items, including salmon, oysters, eggs, and milk. Further, sharks can be cleaned and dressed for table use much more easily than many other kinds of fishes. There is only the spinal column and that is cartilage which cuts readily with a knife.

Shark meat is white and bone free, and it can be prepared in many ways. As steak it can be broiled. It can be cut into serving-size pieces or fish sticks and fried. It can be cooked in a fish chowder; or it can be boiled, flaked, and served in a seafood cocktail. It also can be baked and served with various sauces. Smoked, it is a delicacy. The manner in which shark meat can be served is limited only by the cook's imagination.

Modern scientific developments have opened the door on a great new food use for shark meat. This use, strange as it may seem, is as flour.

Experiments in producing flour from the flesh of fishes have been carried on for a long time. It was proved that it could be done, but the problem lay in completely eliminating a fishy flavor. One of the first times it finally was accomplished was in South Africa, when investigators at a fisheries research institute succeeded in producing a non-fishy-tasting flour from a local species known as mossbunker. Since then a similarly tasteless fish flour has been produced in the United States.

This fish flour has two very important advantages. Being protein rich, it is nutritious. Also, it can be produced in mass quantities at low cost, making wholesale distribution to poverty-stricken, protein-starved peoples throughout the world possible and practical.

The potential of sharks as food is an enormous, largely untapped resource. It seems safe to say that all the sharks caught commercially and by sport-fishermen throughout the entire world are only a fraction of those that die of old age, not to mention those killed by their fellow sharks and, as infants, by other hungry predators in the sea. Once sharks have greater acceptance as human food, a vast new department

Left: The bolo is decorated with a fossilized shark tooth, the key ring on the left with the side tooth of a mako, the key ring on the right with a blue shark tooth, and the tie tack wih a tiger shark tooth

Gordon Rynders

Below: The front fang of a mako dangles from a chain and a tiger shark tooth adorns the tie clasp. Fashioned by Frank Mundus of Montauk, New York.

Gordon Rynders

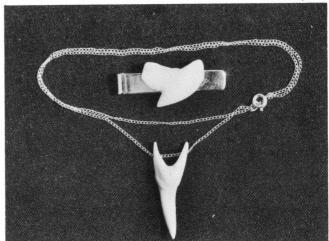

will be opened in the ocean "meat market."

Over the years sharks have been caught commercially in a number of different ways. One of the simplest is a single line carrying a baited hook. When a shark seizes the bait and is hooked, he is hauled in hand over hand. However, commercial fishing requires quantity to be worthwhile, and two of the more productive methods are long-lines and gill nets. A long-line unit consists of a main line about one-half mile long made up of connected sixty foot lengths of nylon rope. Each end of the line is anchored at buoys which hold the line and mark its position. Anywhere from ten to twenty-three hooks attached to branch lines are suspended from the mainline at regular intervals. Periodically the lines are checked, sharks removed, and the hooks baited again. Some commercial fishermen employ as many as twenty of these long-line sets at a time. In the gill net method the nets are designed to trap sharks by their gills. These large nets are set out, anchored, and marked with buoys in places where sharks are numerous. When the sharks collide with the nets they become stuck head first in mesh, and their gill slits prevent them from backing out. Often the trapped sharks become panicked and try to force their way through the nets, a foolish maneuver which causes them to be held more securely. Both methods, long-lining and gill netting, can account for large numbers of sharks.

One other interesting use of shark products is the manufacturing of unique items. Captain Frank Mundus fashions shark teeth into necklaces, tie clasps, earrings, and bracelets. He also imbeds them in clear plastic as novel paperweights. The jaws, with teeth in place, are mounted to make fishing trophies and interesting displays for educational and decorative purposes. Shark heads, and even whole specimens, are mounted for the same purposes. Captain Mundus has the mounted head of a 4,500-pound maneater he captured off Amagansett, New York, which he uses as an exhibit in sportsmen's shows.

Sharks, undoubtedly, will continue to serve mankind in many ways. A particularly exciting way, and one with promise, lies in the field of medical research.

Already Japanese scientists have discovered a method of extracting insulin from the pancreas of sharks for victims of diabetes. Also from the pancreas they derived pancreatin, a substance that aids digestion. Recently, an American neurosurgeon was conducting a series of experiments with sharks in the Bahamas in an effort to locate clues to the causes and prevention of brain damage in humans, such as strokes and head injuries.

It has been stated by one school of scientific thought that sharks do not get cancer, whereas other kinds of fishes do. The statement has been disputed, but if true it poses interesting possibilities. Assume that sharks are not afflicted with cancer; conceivably, shark medical researchers may come across a clue to a cure or even prevention of cancer. Similarly, other medical studies of sharks may point the way to cures for nervous ailments, eye disorders, and the diseases of human organs.

Sharks, although they have been a menace to man, are entering a new era in which, through the efforts and knowledge of scientists, they are fast becoming an aid to man in his conquest of disease and hunger. The further man explores the seas of the world and the inhabitants of these seas the better will humanity be served.

INDEX